I0492209

TURNING
TABLES

DECIDE TO BECOME A BETTER LEADER AND INSPIRE
YOUR TEAM TO CUSTOMER SERVICE SUCCESS

By R. Sinanan
Copyright 2018
Published by Lotus Training

ABOUT THE AUTHOR

Rachel successfully been in the Customer service industry (predominantly the Hospitality industry) in the UK, Australia, Indonesia and Vietnam. Her career has spanned over thirty successful years within the industry, and she is now an author, public speaker and founder of Lotus Training and Crackpots Food Co.
This book has been written with the intention of giving some insight into how to be a better leader, bringing your teams to success and creating success in your business and career in the Customer Service industry.

Rachel can be contacted via her Facebook page www.facebook.com/lotustrainingvn or her website www.rachelsinanan.com

MESSAGE FROM THE AUTHOR

No, I am not one of those people who has climbed Mt Everest, or one of those people who has made millions of dollars building a successful empire. I am also not someone who has studied about motivation, or how to inspire people. This book is just my honest 'learnings' from over the years.

My learning came on the job, I learnt the hard way, making many mistakes along the way, I have failed and won, but ultimately, after learning on the job on how to grow myself and my teams around me, and learning from my mistakes, I made myself successful. At the beginning of my career, I became a Leader without any management experience at all. In my career, I have travelled the world, raised my son whilst travelling, working and living overseas and made some good and bad decisions along the way. I wrote this book to help others who might be making the same mistakes I made over the years, and I hope to save others the heartache of 'silly' mistakes when trying to inspire yourself and the teams around you. Not that I know everything either, I am still learning every day.

Welcome to the career learnings of my life...

Rachel

TABLE OF CONTENTS

INTRODUCTION

Backtrack to 1992, I had just turned twenty-three, and I had been offered a role to manage a business. I had already been working at the venue for a couple of years, but as a bar attendant and helping with the marketing of the business.

I of course accepted the role...then the panic set in. What did I actually know about managing the business. What did I know about leading a team?

Well, quite frankly....nothing.

I started out as a manager who was afraid to delegate, I was afraid to let the teams make decisions for themselves. I wanted everything to be done the way I wanted it done. I did not take any advice given to me by the teams on how to resolve any issues, and I truly believed I knew best.

This, of course, did not work. I learnt the hard way, working myself into the ground and working every hour under the sun to try to make the business work.

I dealt with many customer complaints, many unhappy team members and an unhappy bottom line profit.
I was not utitilising my best assets to grow the business.

MY TEAMS

Over the years, I gradually became better a better leader, and did not have to work myself into the ground. I empowered my teams to success. I learnt how to communicate with my teams on a better level, and now with Millennials making up majority of the Customer service industry workforce, it became even more important to become a better leader.

What have I learnt over the years...

You need to earn the Respect of the Team

Having the ability to show respect, empathy, and care to those that follow you, are all attributed to being a great leader. Earning respect is crucial to a successful relationship with someone, while also showing that you care about their work or ideas. Being empathetic allows a leader to tap into the emotions of that individual in order to connect in a way that lets that person know you understand what it means to be in their situation. Combining all three of these traits can definitely make someone a great leader. These are things you need to constantly work on.

Have a great vision that you can explain…and get buy in from your teams. An unclear vision does not motivate a team…it confuses them.

Did you know over 87% of Millennials expect to be in company that provides opportunities for them to grow?

Gone are the days where it is acceptable to just put someone into a role and expect them to perform well for both you and the business. You need to offer more than just a paycheck.

A great leader knows that the team is what will lead them to success.

They surround themselves with great people that they can cultivate into a team of competent, confident individuals who can work well as a team.

They then have the ability to guide this team towards a well-defined vision by clearly communicating short and long terms goals, inspiring confidence and trust among colleagues, and influencing common efforts through character rather than by a position of authority.

DECIDING TO BECOME A BETTER LEADER

Any team cannot be inspired to success without a good leader. It has to become a conscious decision on your behalf to make this the first step in leading and inspiring your teams.

There is so much written about what makes a bad leader, and the list could be endless, but I believe the following are things that we can recognize at least one in ourselves, and it is up to us as Leaders to try to improve and change this within ourselves to become truly effective leaders and be able to inspire our teams to success.

There are also so many 'tests' which can be done (and are done by many companies) to look into if you are a good or bad leader. These tests can be insightful, but as they are usually done in sterile environments, I do not believe they give a true indication of the person being tested.

The true test is in the real world.

Do you recognize yourself in any of the following?

A 'know it all' -   We all like to think we 'know best' and sometimes the people giving us advice 'must not know what they are talking about.' Most will do this without realizing they are doing it. The best leaders are acutely aware of how much they don't know. They will try to learn and grow with the teams and the business.

Poor communication skills – You know the type, they expect you to 'read their mind' and know what they want without explaining it properly. They tend to send short emails, almost coded so no-one can understand, and then take out their frustration on everyone around them when things are not done the way they wanted them.

Self centered – It is all about them, they want to succeed, but only to further themselves. They usually are authoritarian and do not communicate with their teams or their customers well.

They are unethical and will 'do anything' to get the job done – Yes, some of these leaders do become successful. But would you want to work with them/for them or employ them?

No Vision – If a leader lacks vision, then how do they expect the team to feel at all inspired about anything? They will not know which direction the business is going in, which will lead to a complete breakdown in the team.

Being too tough – Showing a lack of empathy, kindness and humility are not well respected in a leader. You have to be tough to be a good leader, but being overly tough will just end in the team having no respect for you as a leader, or as a person.

Not moving with change – leaders who are too afraid to make any changes, or are too comfortable, and do not want to 'rock the boat' will never improve the business and will find the team around them will become bored. Boredom leads to a lack of interest in the business, and could mean the business loses great team members.

Lacking flexibility – These leaders take the 'one size fits all' type of approach. With the world ever changing and moving very fast, the flexibility of all kinds of businesses is essential for growth. This can be seen regularly nowadays with so many large companies starting to fail, due to 'sitting on their laurels', with the teams around them getting upset and unmotivated because they feel like a 'number', not an individual.

Losing focus – When a Leader loses focus on the priorities, the business is doomed to fail. The team around them will lose focus, and failure for the team is also inevitable.

The culture is wrong – if the leader is unsure of what the culture of the company should be, or has not set a culture, or has set a culture which is negative, can bring down the team morale, which will lead to bad customer service, which in turn puts businesses at high risk.

Blaming everyone but themselves – It happens, no matter how hard you try, sometimes things do not work out the way you need them to to move your business forward. Leaders who blame everyone but themselves will lose respect of not only their team, but also their peers.

Not investing any time in their teams – Yes, you have a lot of work to get done. But if no time is spent on inspiring your team to success, the workload will pile up even more.

Not accepting feedback from customers – Ignoring customer feedback can be very dangerous. Customers need to feel appreciated and important. A leader who ignores a customers feedback cannot expect their team to take any customer feedback on board in the future.

Lack of courage – A good leader will have the courage to lead their teams to success. Lacking courage will ensure the business stagnates and eventually fails.

Did you recognize yourself at all? If you did, it is time to make some changes and DECIDE TO BE A BETTER LEADER.

If you feel yourself 'falling back' into old habits and doing any of the things that can make a bad leader, try to pull yourself out of it. The better the leader, the better the business.

Start to try to do the following, not just once, but everyday all day.

Practice great communication - Discipline yourself to understand what's happening around you by observing and listening. A great leader is always a skilled communicator--not only as speaker but as a listener. Really hear what everyone around you is saying and respond to show you are listening.
Admit when you are wrong - It takes a strong, confident person to say they are wrong. Sometimes people think that admitting you're wrong is a sign of weakness, but in fact just the opposite is true--the more honest and open you are, the more people will respect you as a leader.

Make yourself 'part of the team - There's an acronym that says "team" stands for Together Everyone Achieves More, and great leadership comes from those who see themselves as part of a team, who are willing to roll up their sleeves and do what it takes to support, help, guide and mentor. Hand out Credit to the right people - It's not uncommon to see someone in a leadership position take credit for the work of others, but true leaders are generous with credit. Great leaders will encourage entire teams to be credited for successful work, as it is usually an entire team that has made something wonderful happen.

Become a Mentor at work – As I stated earlier in the book, 87% of millennials want to work in an environment where they can grow. People are interested in growth and development; they want to know how they can do better and find their own path. As a leader your job is to mentor them, guide them and support them--not to boss them or preach to them.

Remember your team is the most important part of the business – *__To be a great leader, you need to start at the heart of what matters in your company--and what matters is your people.__*

If you want to see them happy, engaged, loyal and dedicated, make the time to invest in them, nurture them and provide them with a clear vision of what needs to be done.

Praise your team - Praise people often and openly. Let others know when the work is well done, a job is completed with excellence and the results are great. But, when you need to talk to a team member about something they are doing wrong, do it privately. No-one wants to feel they're being lectured in public. Create a bond between yourself and the team - No, that doesn't mean going for drinks with them every night of the week, it means spending time with the team in the 'trenches' to gain their trust and respect.

Do not spend all the day in the office - Come in early to get your work done early in the morning, or after everyone has left for the day. When everyone else arrives in the morning, get out of your office and connect with people. It's an efficient way to balance the demands of a leadership role, and people feel good about their team when they can see a leader not only working hard but also being available and accessible. It's a win-win.

Don't immediately think the worst - Many of the bad things that happen in the course of a day or a week--a miscommunication, an uncomfortable moment, an act of disrespect--happen because someone is quick to judge and to give their opinion. The best leaders give the benefit of the doubt. They work on being fair and kind and on always giving people a second chance or the benefit of the doubt.

Don't micromanage – Delegate - Leaders who micromanage their teams are stifling their teams, and not allowing them to grow, show their talents and to make best use of their skills. If you want to be a better leader, step back and give people the room they need to do their best.

Build fun into your culture - Business is serious, but the best leaders know how to put some fun and excitement into their culture, creating an optimistic team who are enthusiastic and want to come to work.

Make everyone accountable in their roles - If responsibility and accountability are important to you, don't let those who are slacking get away with it. You more respect from your team by acknowledging if someone in the team is letting everyone down.

Trust them and they will trust you – Trusting your teams and people around you, will ensure they they then can trust you.

Empathise, and show that you care - Leaders who show the most care and understanding of their teams, their customers and their business are more likely to succeed. It builds are respect from your team, and encourages other talents from other companies to want to be part of your team.

Stay happy and enthusiastic every day - Your emotions, if not kept in check in the work environment, can affect not only yourself, but all of those around you. To keep inspiring a team, you must leave your personal problems at home and put any anger you have aside.

Keep growing yourself - If you don't have the skills to lead, no title or position will ever make you into the leader you want to be. There's only one way to become a better leader, and that's to work on your leadership skills, keep developing yourself, and grow what leadership means to you.

Right person right place - Hiring great individuals is only half the game; it's just as important to understand how people of diverse backgrounds and abilities can best work together. Learn to quickly pick up on the gifts and strengths of your people. When you do, you're best equipped to help them build on their strengths and grow the business and the team.

So, what is the most important thing to ensure you are definitely doing everyday?

I believe it is to **have FUN**. A study from BrightHR and leading psychologist Professor Sir Cary Cooper revealed young team members that have fun in the workplace, from belly laughs and birthday celebrations to Xboxes and massages, take less sick leave, work harder and are more productive. Having fun can increase productivity by up to 12%, which for any company is a wonderful thing.

It also encourages other talented persons to want to join your company/team. It reflects in your customer service to the customer, and makes people want to come back.

Having fun with the team and within the work environment does not mean everyone is not focused on what needs to be done, it is quite the opposite. Here are a couple of ideas you can use to ensure your work environment is kept fun.

Socialize offsite monthly - Workplaces where team members and collaborators get along as friends tend to succeed more than places where team members keeps their distance and function as wholly independent operators. Try and keep the socializing events to something everyone can enjoy, and not just a big drinking session, as this can lead to arguments, and destroy what you are trying to achieve.

Celebrate achievements- Most companies have some way of recognizing achievements, such as raises, bonuses, promotions or just nods of recognition. Few offices take the time or effort to celebrate achievements, even major ones. Whenever a team or individual hits a major goal, or when the company reaches a major milestone, treat your team to a real celebration. You don't have to spend a lot of money or take a lot of time, but hosting a mini gathering makes a big impact. It helps people reap the rewards of their hard work, spend time together and feel good about the progress your business has made.

Create Challenges - Friendly competition is always a good thing. You can do this with work challenges -- for example, can award those who make the highest sales for the month with a small party, or divide your team into two teams to see who can achieve the most in a time period. But you can also do this with non-work-related games -- for example, you can sponsor an inhouse sports team. Either way, the competition will get your team members' blood pumping, and will inspire them to work harder in all the other areas of their jobs.

Encourage eating lunch or dinner together as a team - It's so easy to spend all day at your desk, staring at your screen, or dealing with customers but, teams need time to socialize to break up the day. It's important for our minds to take a break, and it's a great way to get to know your team, and for them to see you as more than a "boss".

These are just a few ideas, and I know not all companies have the funds to be able to do what some companies do, such as Twitter who hold meetings on rooftops to keep it interesting, get free meals delivered to the office, give unlimited vacations (for some) and offer mid day yoga classes, but there is always something you can instill into your company that will make it fun and interesting to encourage your team to come to work daily and give their best.

Be the person everyone wants to follow. There are so many benefits to being a Better Leader...here are just a sample:

Motivation

The motivational factor constitutes one of the most important benefits of good leadership in a workplace or company setting. Good leadership within the workplace motivates team members to accomplish more. The potential of the team members or company members under good leadership transforms into performance, which is what every workplace requires.

Confidence

The confidence-boosting factor - another very important benefit of good leadership. The best leaders can create confidence in the individual team members of a company so that the individual team member completes his tasks more efficiently. In addition, good leaders make themselves available to the individuals in their work groups if ever they have questions or need guidance. Knowing that a good leader is always there to guide creates a confidence in team members not seen without proper leadership.

Creates Harmony

Great leaders align company goals with the goals and interests of the individual team members. It also shows a good leader's ability to resolve conflicts within a company amongst different groups of people within. The best leaders can create a special sort of harmony between team members and the owners or operators of a company or company.

Enthusiasm

Good leaders in a company or company workplace will always demonstrate enthusiasm about the work that they do and about their own place in the company or company as a leader. This enthusiasm becomes an added source of motivation for a large majority of individual team members in the workplace, improving their production rates and overall work performance. Enthusiastic leaders promote work groups working towards a common goal and the overall improvement of the work environment.

Talent follows you

Great talent will follow you and want to work with you in future endevours. We all remember those moments in life when we have had a great 'boss' and wanted to stay working with them.

What will you do today to become a better leader?

WHAT IS CUSTOMER SERVICE?

Start with do you know what you are selling? No, I don't just mean getting to know your products (which you should know, that should be a given for you and your team), I mean the experience you are selling i.e how you make your customers feel. If it was just about the products, everyone would pay a great deal less and just buy all their products for a quarter of the price from a cheap competitor.

Customer service is listed in the Oxford dictionary as 'The assistance and advice provided by a company to those people who buy or use its products or services.'

However, in todays' ever-changing world, where customer expectations are at the highest they have ever been, with everyone wanting things immediately and quickly, you need to do more than this to be able to achieve growth within your business and to keep your customers.

Customers will not stand for slow service, slow answers on questions or for incorrect information. We live in an ever-evolving world, where customers can 'google' for answers, before they even ask you and your teams. No, 'googling' does not always give the right answers, but it does make more and more customers feel that they are an authority on anything and everything you sell and do.

Take for example the trend in cooking shows, such as Masterchef. People watch these shows at home and believe that they can become experts in what it takes to be a chef. We all do it, we all watch shows like this and think we know best...

On the other hand, if you are a chef in a busy kitchen, you know that what they air on a cooking show is not the reality of the kitchen in a commercial environment. However, the customers will come in and want to show their knowledge to the people they are with, which can cause problems for the chef, however, unless you are Gordon Ramsey, you have to bite your tongue and try to ensure the customers' expectations are exceeded. This is in all of us. We all do similar things at different stages, different situations, but we all like to show how knowledgeable we are.

The customer experience is one of the most important part of the basics to get right and one of the hardest. It is how you react to the customer and

It is how the customer reacts to their experience that make your business a success or failure.

I have found that excellent customer service involves meeting and surpassing expectations. It means showing the customer how important he or she is to you and the business by interacting with he or she in a friendly- helpful and positive way.

You need to understand your customers' expectations.

- What do they want to gain from becoming your customer?
- What do they expect when they interact with you?
- What would you expect if you were a customer in your own business?

Customer Service is all about how you make the customer feel – how they feel when they are interacting with you and how they feel when they stop interacting with you.

Customer service is not just about when they are in front of you directly, nowadays it covers so many other areas as well.

The way you and your teams respond via email, on the phone, and even in your social life also form a part of your customer service. Word of mouth, through your team or even yourself when socializing, either in person or on Social media can go a long way to either build or destroy your business.

There are so many examples of bad customer service...here are just a few:

- Announcing to the entire store that the customers credit card has been denied. We all know that sometimes our 'failsafe' IT software can have problems, it might not be the customers fault. Even if it is a problem with their card...embarrassing them will not encourage them, or the others that have heard it happen, come back to you.
- Ignoring the customer or delaying their service. This can be one of the worst things to happen. There is nothing more annoying that waiting to be served by someone who might just be chatting with their team members or focusing on something they consider to be 'more important'.
- Not accepting customer feedback. We have all heard the saying 'the customer is always right'. Well, we do know they are not always right, however, it is not up to us to tell them so. Feedback can be helpful in so many ways. It might highlight something you have missed.
- Threatening something bad might happen if they do not use their services. This is not only irritating to customers but can cause stress problems. Not what you need people to think about your business.

- Presenting inaccurate information. This seems to happen more and more, especially in our Social media world. It is easy for some to give incorrect information, and when the customer finds out it is inaccurate, this will cause them to lose respect, not only for the business, but for yourself and your teams as well.
- When the team member helping the customer, then states they cannot help, as it is not part of their role, or they are not authorized to help any further. Empowering your team can resolve this issue, which is discussed later in this book.
- Service staff behaving badly in front of customers. This can be something as simple as playing on their phone, right through to arguing with a customer.
- Being rude to customers because they do not want to renew their services with your company. This does not encourage the person to want to stay.

These are just a few examples. I am sure you know of many more you have experienced yourself.

The internet is full of people posting bad reviews about companies. Fewer post about their good experiences. Many customers will not tell you or your team in person after having a bad experience. They are more likely to try to 'get even' and with the simplicity of being able to post a bad review, this has made it easier for the customer to do this.

If you google 'bad customer service' you will see loads of stories, and examples of bad customer service.

However, google 'Great customer service' and it comes up with a list of what you should expect from your teams, hardly any 'feel good' stories at all.

Research from ThinkJar says now that people use their social media more and more to tell others about their experiences, it was shown that 13% of customers will share a negative customer service experience with 15 or more people. On the other hand, 72% of consumers will share a positive experience with 6 or more people.

Let's look at the maths. If you have 100 customers and 13 of them share a negative customer service experience with 15 people each, 195 people hear about negative customer feedback regarding your company, even though just 13 had bad experiences.

Now, say you have 100 customers and 72 of them share a positive experience with 6 people each, 432 people will hear about positive experiences with your company (much more than 72).

How can you start building a great customer service experience?

'Set the culture'

As the Leader it is your responsibility to 'set the culture'. Have you ever had the unfortunate experience where the entire experience was bad?

This comes from the top. Yes, in a company there will be rules, policies and procedures to follow but it is up to you to create the perfect environment for your customers.

The culture should be positive. To set your culture you need to

Define – define what it is that you will accept as a minimum standard within your business. This is something that does not just involve yourself, but also from the team around you. This will ensure they 'buy in' to the culture.

Demonstrate – this is leading by example. If you have set a certain standard, you also need to abide by it. Your team will not follow your standard if they do not see you adhering to it.

Demand – Not in an authoritarian way but ensure that the team around you are aware that anything less than the standard set is not acceptable.

A great way to set your culture, is to create a 'Customer Charter'. Not to create it by yourself, but to have your team come up with different ideas, and to bring it down to ten focus points with your team. This goes a long way to helping create your vision for the company, and to ensure that your team are behind you in every way to make their customer service the best it can be.

Most larger companies create a Customer Charter, not all will have their teams involved in coming up with the Charter, which can mean there is no buy in within their teams. Some larger companies will have a Customer Charter for the company, but then have individual teams/venues/premises within their company come up with their own Customer Charter. This can also be a great way to ensure buy in with each team.

An example of a Customer Charter I have done with one of my teams in a casual restaurant is below:

To always put our customers first
To create a party environment every day and every night
To always acknowledge our customers when they arrive
To always check back on the food to make sure the customer is happy
To always work together as a team, and to be fair to all

To always be smiling!
To always leave our personal problems at the front door
To follow our customer journey agreement without fail every day
To make the customers feel like the most important people in the world.
To have fun!

This had total 'buy in' from the team, as they had come up with it, and as new team members joined us, it was the team around me that had the new team members buy into the Charter. I did not have to do anything about it at all.

My culture had been set from the beginning. I knew I still had a great deal of work to do, but my minimum standard for Customer service had been set.

CREATING AND IMPLEMENTING A VISION

Why have a vision?

Simple. You cannot start planning if you do not know where you are going or you do not know what you want to become in the future. You cannot map out directions if you do not have a destination in sight. You cannot start strategic business planning if you are cannot envision where your business wants to be.

You can liken your company vision to your business' destination. Unfortunately, it is a fact that not all team members are fully aware of where their company is heading and having a vision will rectify that problem. All levels of the company will be kept in the loop, so to speak, and this awareness will give them focus in carrying out their assigned tasks, duties and responsibilities.

What is a Company Vision?
A mission statement is different to a Vision statement- it is intended to clarify the 'what' and 'who' of a company, while a vision statement adds the 'why' and 'how' as well. As a company grows, its objectives and goals may change.

Therefore, vision statements should be revised as needed to reflect the changing business culture as goals are met.

A Vision is what you aspire the company to be.

A vision statement should stretch the imagination while providing guidance and clarity.

It will help inform direction and set priorities while challenging team members to grow. But most importantly, a vision statement must be compelling not just to the high-level executives of your company, but to all team members.

Here are a couple of things to keep in mind when creating your vision statement:

-   Project five to 10 years in the future.

-   Dream big and focus on success.

-   Use the present tense.

-   Use clear, concise and jargon-free language.

-   Infuse it with passion and emotion.

-   Align it with your business values and goals.

-   Have a plan to communicate your vision statement to your team members.

-   Be prepared to commit time and resources to the vision you establish.

A couple of examples are listed below of some great Vision statements, which might help you come up with yours.

1. "To be the fastest growing, most rewarding and most transformative leadership community." – Mandala Leaders
Nick Bradley, Founder, Mandala Leaders
I run Mandala Leaders and one of the key processes we teach business leaders is how to have a clear, engaging and inspiring purpose, strategy and vision. I believe vision statements should be big, bold and engaging and be simple enough for all team members and customers to remember and live by. Everyone involved in the company should also live by the mantra and that customers see, feel and experience this too.

2. "To be the best quick service restaurant experience. Being the best means providing outstanding quality, service, cleanliness, and value, so that we make every customer in every restaurant smile." – McDonald's
Annette Franz, CEO, CX Journey Inc

This is a great vision statement for so many reasons. It's simple, clear, and easy to understand by the team members and management alike. Had McDonald's stopped at "to be the best quick service restaurant experience," it wouldn't have been a good vision statement because it would've been to generic . Adding an explanation of what it means to be the best sets a clear tone for team members about what is expected. It's also realistic and achievable. Your vision statement should motivate and inspire; if it's not realistic or achievable, it will do neither.

3. Build the best product, cause no unnecessary harm, use business to inspire and implement solutions to the environmental crisis." – *Patagonia Andrew Schrage, Founder & CEO, Money Crashers* It's a great vision statement because it is brief and to the point. It speaks of the values it possesses as a company and the value it brings to its customers and the environment in general. It also gives its customers a sense of connection, something all vision statements should have.

A Vision statement should be a 'living and breathing' document. Not something that is just written and forgotten about as time goes on.

You should be willing to change it and help it evolve as the business changes and evolves. This encourages your teams to stay enthusiastic and encourages them to grow with the business and the Vision for the business.

The benefits of a clear vision statement to a company can be enormous. A clear vision statement defines the direction the company is going, sets the stage for strategic plans, and shows exactly what a company "stands for". It can also provide other significant benefits for your teams.

Benefit one – A clear vision statement acts as a 'binder' for your team and has a positive impact on company effectiveness. When teams understand and buy-in to the company's vision statement, it brings them together. It focuses efforts so everyone is working towards the same understood goal.

Benefit two – A solid vision statement acts as a guide for team actions and decision making. For example, if there is a decision to be made to undertake a project, or how to take action on a task: simply stop and ask, "Is what I am doing consistent with our company's vision statement?" If it is, great, move forward. If not, or if there is any doubt, now is the time to pause, evaluate, and if need be, tie the action or decision with the vision statement; or not do it. The vision statement will provide the guidance teams need to make the right decisions.

Benefit three – Possibly the greatest benefit of a clear vision statement is it can be motivating and inspiring. When an individual understands the vision of the company, they are able to readily commit to, and engage in, the company's efforts. Engaged and inspired teams can go a long way in helping the company achieve its mission and goals, it helps the teams achieve their own personal goals and can help you achieve your goals in your own career.

So, you need to write your Vision statement, ideally following the steps below:

Step 1: Set a time frame
How long is the time period within which you expect to achieve the goal that you have envisioned? There is no fixed time frame for this purpose, although most businesses – even startups – tend to think long-term. Normally, time frames are for 5 years and 10 years. Others even reach 20 and 30 years. Some even break down their Vision to 'yearly snippets' to help the team realise the goals and the vision. It really depends on what type of business you are in.

Step 2: Write the first draft
This is considered by many to be the most difficult part of creating a vision statement: getting started.

Come up with a dream that you have for the business. Adopt a "dream big" attitude. We all have them. I have been sitting in my kitchen, cooking products, getting up at 5am to get orders out, and all the while, knowing that in the future, I will have large teams around me to do this, as I grow the business.

Your dream has to be huge, it has to be something incredible, and it has to be something really bold. In fact, at first glance, it may even seem unattainable. That's perfectly all right. It is what you envision, after all.

When developing your Vision, you have to be specific, clear and concise about it. Anyone who reads your Vision should be able to understand it completely when they first look at it. Your objective is for your vision to come across without any need for questions or clarifications.

Have a future-oriented mindset. Pretend that it is already the future, and you are already at the end of the time frame that you have previously set. Here, you assume that have already achieved your company vision.

Before putting it into words, take into consideration the following:
- The size of the company;
- The company structure;
- The company's claim to fame.

- What do you want the company to be famous for?

- Your specific goals for measuring success;
- The kind of people needed by the company, including their qualifications and skill sets;
- The attitude of the members of the company towards their jobs, the company, and their working environment;
- What the company will and will not do;
- The personal thoughts and feelings of the business owner or founder towards the business;
- The most important offerings of the company to customers or clients;
- Public perception of your business.

Step 3: Get feedback

The best people to get the most relevant feedback from are those that will be implementing it: Your Team, from top management to the team members. This helps give them ownership of the Vision, which in turn makes your job very easy. Have your outline first, but take the feedback and work with it. The pride your teams will have when they have been able to help with something that is historically 'the big bosses' job will show in all of your customer service transactions moving forward.

Step 4: Rewrite

Unless you are a seasoned "company vision creator or writer", you are bound to encounter a need to do rewrites. Use the feedback you have been given. It is very easy to let our ego's take over, and want to write it ourselves, but the best Vision statements can come from entire teams within a company.

Step 5: Get feedback on the rewrite

Steps 4 and 5 may be done repeatedly, until such time that you are satisfied with the vision you have created.

Step 6: Share the vision

The final company vision must then be shared to those within your teams.

Sharing the Vision

How you share the Vision can also make or break your teams' enthusiasm to make the Vision a reality. I have seen so many companies over the years who put their company vision into their introduction package when someone joins a company, and then never follow it up. When a team member joins the company, they have so much they have to learn and to get used to, the company vision might not be something they remember.

I have worked for companies for long periods of time, one company I worked for over six years, and I still do not know what their Vision was.

I would ensure my Venue had its own Vision, but the company Vision...who knows. I am sure it was in the handbook they handed out when you first joined. I am also sure that over the six year period I was with them they must have updated their Vision, but it was never communicated properly to the teams running the Venues.

A good Vision statement becomes part of your daily life within the company. It ensures that it is something the team lead their daily work life to aspire to get the company to achieve the dream laid out in the vision statement.

Following these steps can help you achieve full 'buy in' to your Vision statement:

Make sure the vision is more than a framed document hanging on the wall or a page in your Induction. Teams are more likely to act off what they see in the those around them versus what they read on the wall. It's not good enough for senior leaders to develop a powerful vision. They need to make sure that the vision is clearly communicated to every team member, along with the goals that will help bring the vision to life. When people are clear on their destination, and are given a map to get there, as well as a tour guide communicating along the way, they will not only support the expedition, but usually will really enjoy the trip.

Meet often. Every Monday Steve Jobs would meet with his executive management team to discuss strategy and current projects and on Wednesdays he would meet with his marketing and communications team. It's not always necessary to hold meetings this often but it is important to keep the lines of communication open.

Be Positive and make yourself 'contagious' in delivery of the Vision Statement. Your attitude, when delivering the message, will in a large part determine the response of your team members. If you present the idea as positive and exciting, your team members will be more positive in their response. If you express doubt, we guarantee you that your team members will quickly support you in finding ways to prove that "it" won't work and is just another one of management's off the wall ideas.

Place a high value on two-way communication. Get in the habit of actively seeking your teams' thoughts and opinions, especially prior to making decisions that impact their work. You'll experience fewer surprises along with greater team engagement and productivity if you consistently encourage your teams to think and provide their input to help you and your team make the best decisions possible.

Over-communicate. In this global market place, keeping pace requires change after change. Most teams understand that to be successful, plans will frequently change. What they don't like is being blindsided because they did not know that the plan had changed. Make it a high priority to provide timely updates when plans change.

Choose your words carefully. Know your audience and appreciate their background and level of understanding. While you would never knowingly "talk down" to teams, make sure that the examples you use and the words you choose are understandable and appropriate. Words and concepts that you routinely use in management circles may not be the right ones to use when talking with teams. Check for understanding and make adjustments to your delivery, when needed.

Great leaders do a great job of communicating Vision statements. Make it your personal responsibility to tell the right people, the right information, at the right time – all the time.

CREATING THE TEAM

So far we have talked about you deciding to become a better leader, the meaning of customer service and the Vision statement. Once all of these things are in place, it is time to 'Create your team'.

Yes, in most roles you will 'inherit' an existing team.

This does not mean you have to keep things the way they 'have always been' (although, many teams will initially 'baulk' at any change, due to the fear of the unknown, and not knowing you).

Lets start with the basics. ***Get to know them.*** Really get to know them. Focus on what drives them, and make sure they are aware of what drives you, and why you are there.

Your team needs to respect you before you get any real 'buy in', and this is earnt, not just given. The respect will come initially from trust.

To build trust you will need to do the following (some of which we have already discussed)

Communication – open communication between yourself and the teams will ensure a 'two way street' and ensure the team understand what is needed/required in their roles and what to expect from you.

Honesty – never lie to them. This can be problematic if there is 'rumours' about the business and you cannot for some reason give the teams the truth (for example, something about to be announced to shareholders), but apart from those types of things, you must at all times be honest with them.

Open your ears – listen to them. Really hear what the teams are telling you. You need to be able use their feedback to be able to grow the business and yourself.

Praise the teams – there is nothing worse than leaders who only speak when something is wrong. Praise can be something as small as a 'thank you so much for doing …..'. It can make a team members day, and encourage them to focus on what is important, your customers.

Ask the team for ideas – this motivates teams. It makes them really feel a part of the company, and not just living in a 'dictatorship'.
Give them open and honest feedback. No, not in front of the rest of the team, this might make them feel 'little'. Sometimes your best team members are just in the right role at the time, and just need to be moved into the right one.

Getting to know your team does not mean you need to socialize with them all the time or go round to their house every weekend. It is about learning more about each member of your team, their skill sets, how they are motivated and their likes and dislikes.

This knowledge is invaluable to leaders, as it allows them to match each team member's expertise and competencies to specific problems, which will help increase their productivity and job satisfaction.

As well as this, try to include your team members in the decision making process where possible. Give your team's open-ended projects and allow them to determine the best solution. This will encourage them to cooperate and develop problem solving skills.

Build relationships between your team members as well. As your team starts to cooperate more, examine the way they work together and take steps to improve communication, cooperation and trust amongst the team. If there are any conflicts, try to resolve them amicably. There is a chapter towards the end of this book about managing conflict which will help with this as well. Listen to both sides of the argument and act as a mediator. One way to do this is to brainstorm solutions, which helps to empower your teams and may lead to new solutions to the problem.

Once you have established relations with and between your team members, it's time to help them work together effectively. Encourage your team to share information, both amongst themselves and within the wider company. Also, try to communicate more with your team.

This goes beyond simply holding meetings, and includes things like being open to suggestions and concerns, asking about each team member's work and offering assistance where necessary, and doing everything you can to communicate clearly and honestly with your team.

You also need to set your ground rules so you can begin officially establishing your team through creating team values and goals, as well as evaluating team performance alongside individual performance.

Be sure to include your team in this process, so they know what's required and agree with it.

Not setting and enforcing ground rules within the business can result in the rest of the team losing motivation and not giving the service to your customers that you need them to, to achieve your Vision.

We all live within a certain set of rules in our businesses. Virtually every company has a policies handbook that is given to every new team member.

One of the activities I've often done as with a new team is to let the team establish their own set of ground rules. We usually write them out on a page of flip-chart paper and hang it up in a staff area.

Examples of team ground rules

Some of the types of rules I've seen teams establish are:

No Whining – This helps to create a more positive culture within the team. If someone starts to complain or become negative in any way, team members can point to the list and call the whiner out.

Always be on time – Some team members just want to say "Be on time." I like to word it this way to remind people why it is so important.

Everyone contributes – We've all been in that group project in school where that one person just coasts along on everybody else's work. If you haven't, maybe you're that guy.

Silence indicates agreement – Some people like to sit on the fringes without ever providing an opinion. Then when things fail, they say that they were against it all along. A rule like this helps to ensure that people are engaged.

These are only some suggestions. Team ground rules vary based on the individuals that make up the team. The focus should be on making sure people are team players.

Some other suggestions you can use to help when establishing a list of team ground rules:

Try not to target specific persons within the team. If some people on the team have an issue with one individual, creating a rule directed at them could be counter-productive. For instance, if someone has a hygiene issue or has an offensive smell, it's best to deal with them individually rather than creating a team-wide rule for them.

Be positive. **This should be part rules, part fun. I've seen team ground rules like, "Take turns bringing sweets in for the entire team'** Try to establish rules that focus on what the team should do rather than what they should not be doing.

Know your objectives for creating your ground rules. Establishing team ground rules accomplishes a number of objectives:

They create a positive environment: Team ground rules should be part serious business and part fun. They are designed more to generate a team culture than to keep people in line.

They encourage your team to 'self manage': Team members are encouraged to enforce the rules in more of a peer pressure environment.

Rules makes the team more productive: Establishing team ground rules is a way to write down the unwritten rules. The team is more productive when there's a friendly reminder to be on time and respect each other's' space.

They help bond your team together: Hopefully the individuals will feel more like part of the team, which should bring the team closer together.

Establishing team ground rules at the beginning is a great way to establish a strong culture among team members. The concept is more about establishing a team than setting down rules.

Hopefully the team will have fun with it and create a few inside jokes with each other in the process.

Team building is one of the most important responsibilities a leader has. It isn't something that can be achieved in a short time and then forgotten. It is an ongoing organic process that you a will have to work on and guide. As this process unfolds, however, your team members will begin to trust and support one another and share their skill sets and effort in order to more effectively complete companies and your personal goals.

What if you have to build a completely new team?

Well, that will start with writing the advertisement.

When writing your advert take into account everything you are looking for. It is important to be clear as to what you want and need.

Ask yourself the following questions
- Do you need a particular type of person to balance your team?
- Do you want them to come to you with experience, or would you rather train them yourself?
- What message about your business do you want to get across to your potential candidates?
- Remember to attract the best, you need to have the best job advertisement. So many people rush this part of the recruitment process, without realising that the way a position is advertised reflects directly on the company and yourself.
- Once you have placed your ad...you are then looking to sift through your applicants, and to organise interviews.

Interviews can be laborious without a plan. Some people you organise to interview will not turn up, some will be late (is this the type of person you really want in the business)? Some will have lied on their CV's. So, make sure you are asking the right questions...again, an example of some interview questions are on the next page.

What circumstances brought you to apply for this role?

How would your best friend describe you?

Why did you leave your last role?

Tell me about a time you went above and beyond to get a job done.

Tell me about a time you had to resolve a conflict, either with another team member or with a customer.

If you could find the 'perfect job' for you...what would it be and why?

What do you know about this business/company?

Of course, your interview questions are not limited to these, but the answers given should give a good overview of the person you are interviewing.

You always need to ensure you balance your team, and that they also compliment you.

For teams that are going to provide customer service, I have found the key was to hire on their personality traits rather than their skills.

If a person's personality and interpersonal skills seem right, then does past experience become relevant to the discussion? Hiring teams that display empathy, curiosity, grit, and the willingness to work together as part of a team will help ensure the success of your customer focused business.

These types of team members are guaranteed to be more motivated and their hard work will definitely be a plus for your company.

Personality traits shine through in particular customer service examples, such as this one from the Ritz Carlton Hotel.

Hotel chain Ritz-Carlton showed an example of excellent customer service in 2012, when Chris Hurn's family went on holiday to one of the hotels in Florida. On return from their holiday, the family discovered that their son's beloved stuffed giraffe toy had been left behind. In order to pacify the upset child, Chris told his son that Joshie the giraffe was simply taking a long holiday at the hotel. That night, the Ritz-Carlton called Chris to say that they had Joshie and would return him as soon as possible. To Chris' young son's surprise, Joshie was returned in a package containing extra goodies as well as a series of photographs of Joshie on holiday around the Florida resort!

This was not from people who were skilled in making this happen, this was a personality trait of the person who initiated the response.

Now, apart from all of this, there is something that is so important...and so many dis-regard it.

TRAINING...

Training your teams and coaching them. This should be ongoing. As I said before, 87% of Millennials want to be able to grow and progress within their own roles.

There are so many benefits to training and coaching. These are just a few of the benefits when doing ongoing training - whether you are a business who wants to train your team members, or you are someone who wants to personally improve and grow.

Personal development is a "process of self-education aimed at enhancing professional skills, employability, quality of life, self-discipline, talent and potential". For anyone hoping to climb the career ladder or improve their sense of purpose, personal development is invaluable.

Businesses can benefit by:

Keep up with industry changes
Industries are constantly changing and so it is important for a business to develop to avoid being left behind. It's also important to make sure your business is complying with any industry regulations, which can be achieved through ongoing training, making sure your staff's skills and knowledge are up-to-date.

Staying ahead of competitors
Standing still can kill your business, so by making sure your staff are constantly advancing, you will continue to move forward are remain competitive within the marketplace.

Be able to see weaknesses and skill gaps
With regular training, a business can more easily identify any gaps in the market and skill gaps within the existing workforce. By identifying these gaps early, there is time to train staff in these required areas so they can fulfil the role effectively.

Maintain knowledge and skill
Although one off training may be provided to new starters, or other team members, it's important that training schemes are put in place to help develop skills throughout their job. To retain knowledge, skills need to be practiced and refreshed on a regular basis so elements aren't forgotten.

Advance team member skills
Once a business has spent money on providing basic level skills, these can easily be built upon and improved to provide much more benefit to the business. Staff that know more can bring more to the table, and your business will reap the rewards.

Provide an incentive to learn
If training is provided as part of a longer development pathway, team members will have much more incentive to learn, participate in the session and put their new skills into practice. Increase job satisfaction levels

Through continued investment from the business, staff can have a much higher sense of job satisfaction, which can improve their motivation towards their work. ***This reduces team member turnover and increases productivity, which directly improves the profitability***. It also prevents competitors from taking away your best team members by offering training incentives.

Provide internal promotion opportunities
Employing new team members involves high recruitment costs and hiring fees. However, with ongoing training, your existing teams can become more eligible for internal promotions. Unlike new team members, you can guarantee they have a complete knowledge of your business, the correct skill set and are people that you know and trust.

Attract new talent
All businesses want to have the best team members and so with ongoing training, this will not only mean better staff retention, but the business may also attract better talent from the start, as this gives the business a good image and is a key feature many people look for within their job search.

Training teams should not be a 'one off'. It should be ongoing, and you should offer variation on what is being trained, to keep the team inspired and motivated.

An un-trained team can destroy customer focused businesses, it reflects badly not just on the team member, but the entire business and the rest of the team.

All in all, you cannot just 'create a team' and forget about it. The team around you is what will make your business a success and it is important to remember to nuture your team daily, inspire them daily and they will bring your Vision to life.

SETTING THE STANDARDS

You have created your team, put your Vision into place and hopefully set up a Customer charter. So, what is next.

First step is to understand your Customer expectations.

Customer expectations have evolved over time, but never as rapidly as they have in the past couple of years.

We can thank (or blame) technology for most of these new customer expectations. The amount of information that's available at the speed of light and in the palm of people's hands makes nearly everyone expect more.

Customer service decision-makers want to meet those expectations — at least in concept. Nearly 95% of leaders (Entreprenuer 2018) say providing a good customer experience is their top strategic priority, according to recent Forrester research. Three-quarters of them want to use customer experience as a competitive advantage.

To them, the idea and intent looks great on paper. The actual implementation is quite a bit different. You see, many don't have the means to improve the experience in the ways customers expect them to.

Just 37% of leaders have a dedicated budget for customer experience improvement initiatives, according to Forrester research.

With or without a budget geared toward meeting expectations and improving the customer experience, leaders need to know what customers want now and how it will drive their satisfaction and loyalty. Then they can focus efforts on meeting expectations and driving results.

Current Customer expectations include the following:

Expectation No. 1: More personalisation

It's kind of ironic that in the far-reaching online world we have all come to love, in which so many business and personal interactions can be anonymous, customers want very personalized experiences.

They expect a company will put the information and products they want where they expect to find them.

Nearly half of consumers will dump their online cart if they can't find a quick answer to their questions.

That means, a customer service rep better be available to chat at any given second customers navigate your website. Or the phone number must be prominently displayed on all web pages so customers don't have to work to find it.

Yes, most customers still want a personal one-on-one experience. Take, for example, a small-industry specific study: Wells Fargo found 60% of banking transactions are made by customers who still prefer to do business with a teller. That's despite the fact that account holders have services available to them online and via mobile devices.

Expectation No. 2: More options

Now that you're thinking about how you can make service more personalised, you might as well add a Part B to that list.

Customers want self-service, voice, digital and social means to interact with a company and its people — and they still expect each to deliver a personalised experience.

Face to face interaction is still the most preferred tool, which makes sense when you consider that talking to a knowledgeable, kind person who is helpful is about as personal as you can get.

Still, in the past three years, the use of other channels has risen:
Web self-service — 18%
Online communities — 39%, and
Chat — 43%.
(Forbes 2018)

While offering as many channels to communicate as customers demand is important, it's probably more vital that communication is easy for the customer.

Expectation No. 3: Constant contact
The majority of customers don't find advertising, promotions and "just touching base" as a nuisance. They expect some follow-up efforts to fill in their customer experience. It's a request that can benefit business as well. Keeping in touch can deflect incoming contacts, which can reduce costs and boost customer satisfaction and revenues.

The key is to give them the right amount of information at the right time through the channel they prefer. So before businesses increase (or start) outbound communication, they want to involve customers. That boils down to finding out:

- What customers want to hear from you
- When they want to hear from you, and
- The channel(s) they want you to use.

Expectation No. 4: Listen and respond quickly
Good news: Most customers don't find your surveys and other requests for feedback annoying (unless, of course, you bombard them constantly). Customers' biggest expectation in the feedback loop is that companies do something with what they have to say.

Companies need to respond to feedback, act on it and let customers know what's been done to make their experience better based on the data. If not, customers will cease to give feedback.

Expectation No. 5: Empower your team
Customers' tolerance for jumping through hoops has become something that now is a real 'no-no'.

Customers now believe they should have what they want the minute they request it.

That's why customers expect teams to be knowledgeable enough to handle anything — and have the authority to do what needs to be done to satisfy customers.

Companies often fail to give their teams this authority because all they think about is the small percentage of customers aiming to take advantage of them.

But the reality is most customers have good intentions — they just want their issues resolved, problems fixed and questions answered. Those are things nearly any customer service teams can handle if trained and empowered.

As a leader, you are probably already used to being able to perform to a high standard, and many of your standards you set will come from your own experiences, and experiences you know about from others. It is very important to set your standards and expectations very early in your role as a leader, and to communicate this to your team, so that they know the expectations around their roles.

Every company needs to have boundaries and standards, so customers and your teams know what to expect when working with you.

If your business hasn't already set solid boundaries with your teams and established proper standards for work, it's time to do so. Every company needs boundaries and standards, so customers know what to expect when dealing with you.

Setting Professional Boundaries
When creating a set of boundaries for your business, take problems you commonly experience with your customers into consideration. If you deal with unreasonable customer expectations, add language to your contracts or marketing materials with costs, and timelines you're comfortable setting.

Professional standards include the business's quality of work. Setting standards for your business is essential, as your customers want to know what to expect when doing business with your company.

Standards also help you to gauge the quality of your work to ensure it's up to par and delivers results promised to customers. For example, a weight-loss company might set standards that within a month a client will lose a certain percentage of body fat.

Abiding by standards can help your business grow and improve by not accepting results that don't meet your promises to customers.

When setting professional standards for your company, consider operating principles that are important to you. Use these values to create the criteria you abide by, including how you'll treat clients, how they should treat you and benchmarks regarding the quality of your work. Standards commonly include issues like honesty, integrity, professionalism and taking responsibility for your actions.

I have always tended to hold a team meeting within my first couple of days. This not only helps me to start to get to know the team, but helps them to get to know me, and what my expectations are of the team, the business.

An example of one of my first team meetings is below. I always also put in 'House policies', so that it is very clear what my expectations are. This team meeting was help with a team of young bar and floor staff, who did not necessarily want to be in their roles forever, as majority were students studying full time and working part time, but I still needed the 'buy in' to ensure my business worked:

Welcome, why are we here today?

To make ourselves known throughout the area as one of the best teams around. I realise that many of you want to do other things in your life but working here should be something to be proud of and we need to take pride in our business to be able to move it forward.

Because great service means the customer never has to ask for anything...go the extra mile. You will be surprised at how people remember the little things.

Where do you think the best service is? Why?

For me it was in a cafe, the team member saw me drop my cutlery on the floor and before I got a chance to ask, they had replaced it. Food was average, but I would go back, due to their hospitality

A customer's Minimum expectation is to be made to feel very important – like the most important person in the room.

We should be BETTER THAN AVERAGE...EVERY CUSTOMER, EVERY VISIT.

The start of your shift... (Even if you are starting half way through the day)!
Do you know the specials, is there anything we don't have or are running low on?

Is the bar comfortable – lighting right, is the room at the right temperature?

Are you ready? Have you checked fruit/ice/stock in fridges? Are tables set?

Is music on at the right 'level?'

Do you know how many we have booked in? What promotions do we have on...coming up?

Are tasting notes for beers up?

Do the toilets have toilet roll/soap?

Would you be comfortable coming in here?

Walt Disney – "There is no magic to magic, it is all in the details"

The customer journey

Welcome on arrival – Most important part of the journey. No-one shall be left hovering. Even if busy – a quick smile, hello, 'be with you in minute' 'take a seat, I will be straight over' etc.

Seat at their tables – explaining the specials, explaining how to order (food and drink) and ensuring they all have menus.

All tables should be offered table service.

Drink service – fruit in all, wedges of lime in soft drinks/white spirits, wedges of lemon in dark – exclude bourbons and whiskeys. All spirits/wines should be measured. Don't be afraid to use loads of ice. It presents the drink better!

Offering a tab – to stop the customer having to pay at each transaction.

Taking the food order – do they want any extra sides, do they want to order any desserts?

Taking the food to the table: do they have the right cutlery (e.g. steak knives), when giving them their food – they should always be told to enjoy their meals.

Walking the floor – do not ignore the customers – smiling – using lines such as 'I trust your enjoying your meals' creating a personal relationship.

Clearing the starters – have you called mains away to the kitchen? If only half a large table has ordered starters – call mains away earlier (half way through the starters).

Have you consistently offered more drinks?

Communication is key...keeping the communication lines open between the kitchen and the customer – if there is a delay on food – the customer should be apologised to and kept informed. A customer should never have to chase us down to ask us what is going on. Communication will prevent problems occurring.

Has their journey been a good one? Have they left with the right feelings? (They had such great service, they want to come back?)

We should always be aware of the customers' needs – even when doing things such as making coffee...not ignoring the customer – it takes two seconds to acknowledge the customer and let them know you will be with them in a minute.

House Policies
The following House policies have been put into place to ensure a safe and happy working environment for all team members.
Not abiding by the house policies, will result in disciplinary action.
Availability
You must notify your manager if you require days off for personal reasons a minimum of two weeks prior.
Sickness
A minimum of two hours' notice must be given to the manager if you are unable to attend your shift due to illness.
Start and End of Shift
It is not acceptable to be late for the start of your shift or to leave your shift early. If you are held up and are running late, you must ring and notify the Manager. You cannot sign off from your shift until the manager tells you it is OK to do so.

The start time on your shift means that you are ready to work at this time with the correct uniform on, and smile on your face.

Customers
Customers must always come first. They must never be left looking for help. We must acknowledge them straight away. It is not acceptable to leave them unattended at any time. The customer is the main focus of the restaurant and bar areas. All customers are to be treated like VIP's (Very Important People) at all times.

Breaks
Breaks can only be taken when given by your manager.

Product
Giving away of any food or liquor item (this includes ANYTHING that would normally be rung into the till e.g. soft drinks) is considered theft. Theft results in Instant Dismissal. Under no circumstances is anything to be given away to friends/family/customers without consent from the manager.

I did not run the meeting as a 'lecturer'. This would have made the team 'switch off' during the meeting, and it would have been a waste of time. The standards I set were always the minimum expectation, in this business example I always hired my team more on personality than skills, as it was a fairly simple operation, and personality is not something I believe you can teach.

It takes a special kind of person to be great at Customer service, not all can achieve it, even if they have the technical knowledge.

It is important to get the team involved in the meeting. Ask them for bad experiences they have had as a customer, and why they did not enjoy their experience. Question as you present, this can help check back with them that they have full understanding.

You will also need to set standards for the products you are selling to your customers.

In retail this means that your products need to be displayed well, and your team have to have an understanding of how to display merchandise to ensure the product looks enticing. In hospitality, it covers so much more...the food must be cooked well, and presented well, the drinks must be made correctly and presented well, and the team in both industries must be ready at a moments' notice to drop whatever it is they are doing to help a customer in need.

The same can be said for an office environment. Even if the Customer service is only by phone, do you ensure you team pick up the phone in a set number of rings? Do you ensure they are friendly in their manner on the phone and encourage your customers to ask them questions to secure a deal?

How do you create a set of service standards?

There are at least seven potential sources of information to help define the service standards for a business:
- Management: You should seek information from different levels of management. However, do not rely solely on management input – existing customers are a better source.
- Team members: This group is too often overlooked – 'what do they know?' is a view that has been expressed.

In fact, team members interact with customers every day, so they are a really valuable source of information and will expect to contribute to the process.

- Existing customers: These are a rich source of information. A few focus groups will usually generate an excellent set of customer expectations.
- Potential customers: What can you learn from people who are choosing an alternative supplier?
- Lost or former customers: Why did these customers not return? They will probably be pleased to tell you.
- Competitors: Mystery shopping and monitoring competitors' web sites and literature can reveal useful input.
- Regulatory authorities: The activities of some types of business are governed by a regulator who sets service standards that must adhered to.

How many standards should we have?

You should have standards that are appropriate to the size, diversity and complexity of the business. Initially, I would suggest that you establish a small number of service standards that focus on the absolutely critical areas of your business.

You will need a period of time for your team to 'buy–in' to the concept of service standards, the monitoring arrangements and the benefits of implementing an effective program.

Once they have become a way of life, consider expanding the range of measures on a 'need to have not nice to have' basis.

You should only have service standards that can be monitored accurately and with an appropriate degree of effort.

After having attained the desired service level, the next great challenge faced by service providers is to maintain service standards at levels of excellence.

This is as important, and as tough, as establishing service standards and attaining to them in the first place.

There are basically two approaches that any company can have towards maintaining service standards - a proactive approach or a reactive approach.

Proactive: A proactive approach entails actively reaching out to customers and trying to gather their feedback on service quality and suggested areas of improvement. This can be done by way of

Surveys and administering questionnaires and Staff training

Surveys and questionnaires: Such an approach helps a brand to anticipate customer demands and expectations and align its service offering accordingly. Also, the findings of such surveys can help to identify common issues and demands of customers hence helping a company to customize its service offering.

Team Training: Another crucial aspect of the proactive approach is team training. Companies nowadays spend generously on training their personnel to adequately handle customer queries and/or complaints. This is particularly true if a company is changing its service offering or going in for a price hike of its existing services. For example, when a fast food chain increases the price of its existing products, the staff has to handle multiple customer queries regarding the hike. Lack of a satisfactory explanation would signify poor service standards and lead to customer dissatisfaction.

Reactive: A reactive approach basically consists of resorting to a set 'script' once a customer complains about poor service quality. It usually starts with apologizing to the customer and then taking steps to redeem the situation. The fundamental flaw with this approach is that, here the customer has already had a bad experience of the brand's service.

Social media has allowed many companies to have a 'reactive' approach with their dealings. Some only respond when people tag them for millions to see.

Standards within a business need to be constantly looked at and maintained to try to prevent a 'reactive' action.

Another crucial element to be kept in mind while seeking to maintain service quality is to have in place a metric for 'measuring' quality. The particular guidelines selected would depend on the type of business, service model and the customer expectations.

For example: at a customer service call center of a telecom provider, the way to measure service quality could be the average time taken for handling a call or rectifying a complaint. For a fast food outlet, the way to measure service quality of the sales staff could be the number of bills generated as a percentage of total customer footfalls or the increase in sales month on month.

Many customers use a 'Mystery customer' style measurement to look at their customer service. I have even worked for companies which used this tool as one of the Key performance indicatiors for the management team.

The fault with this type of measurement, is that when you know the questions asked of the mystery customer to answer, it becomes easy to 'spot' your mystery customer, which then the team can work with and provide the best experience. This does not give a true indication of how the business is operating.

Results can become 'skewed' and can in turn, cause a drop in sales as the measurement is incorrect, and gives a false sense of security in that business, which can in turn lead to the business failing.

MAKING THE TEAM FEEL IMPORTANT AND APPRECIATED.

Sounds like an easy thing to do, right? But it is one of the hardest to achieve.

A coaching culture focuses on unlocking the potential of team members at all levels, striving to stretch their roles and giving them new responsibilities.

This approach corresponds much more than the traditional authoritarian management style to the expectations and preferences of millennials who will soon represent the majority of team members worldwide.

Coaching of team members should not be limited to technical skills, but rather embrace a more comprehensive perspective, including personal and social skills, greater awareness and management of emotions, as well as improving interpersonal competencies.

Would you work for a company that does not appreciate you?

You may say that the workplace doesn't seem like the place for positive emotions. And besides, why should you thank your team for doing their job – you're paying them for that, isn't it?

Still, put yourself in your team member's shoes for a second. If your work goes unnoticed and you feel underrated, well that doesn't sound much like a job you'd like to keep at all costs, right? And I know there's plenty of fish in the sea and no team member is irreplaceable but this is not the leader reputation you want. People do talk and rumors spread faster than news and news faster than happenings.

Customer service is not a department. It is a philosophy to be embraced by every team member – from the CEO to the most recently hired.

It still surprises me that many companies don't recognize the value of training their team members – all team members – in the area of customer service.

No, not everyone is trained the same. Someone on the front line, who has direct contact with customers, will be trained differently than someone in the warehouse, who has virtually no contact with a customer.

But here is the point: At some point, everyone is going to impact the customer.

Front-line customer service is obvious. People who interact directly with a customer must have a skillset and mindset to meet or exceed a customer's expectations.

Some of the more important traits and abilities might be friendliness, empathy, communication skills, problem solving, patience and more. Companies spend hours and days – sometimes weeks – training the people on the "front line."

Yet the people who aren't trained are often the people who could have the greatest impact on the customer.

As an example, the warehouse team member who improperly packs a box will create a problem for the customer when the package arrives and the contents are damaged or a part is missing.

Sure, that warehouse team member never talks to the customer, but what he or she does every day, picking and packing products, has a big impact on the customer. At a minimum, the warehouse team member needs to understand the impression the company is trying to create for the customer, and how he or she fits into a culture that is customer-focused. And, that takes training.

Training should start on the first day. There are some companies that won't let an team member start doing what they were hired to do until they receive basic training.

Disney is one of the best examples of this. All team members, also known as cast members, regardless of what they are hired to do, must go through what is called Traditions Training, where they learn the basics of the Disney philosophy, which is genuinely focused on the customer/guest.

Let's start with the first day of a new team members' working life with you as their leader.

They need to have Orientation training. This can be as basic as showing them around your building, introducing them to the team, and discussing the Vision you have for your business. It is a good idea to 'partner them up with someone who has been there for a-while, so they have a 'go to' person when they don't know where something is, or what they should be doing. This works particularly well if you have your current team believing and living the Vision of your company, and understanding the standards and expectations set within your company.

Once Orientation has been done, and the new team member is settled into their role, it is important to keep the momentum going.

Training the team in every aspect to empower them is not only a necessity for your business, but it helps the team to feel important, and gives them a reason to stay on with you.

Step one is to create a Training needs assessment. The basic training needs assessment can be broken down into three parts:

- Use the company vision to help assess the outcome you want from your training. Don't provide training if it's not clear why you're doing it, or if it doesn't directly support the required outcomes. It is a good idea to complete reviews with the team prior to training, to help assess the needs.
- Determine the tasks the team need to perform so the company can reach your company vision, and their personal goals. Ask yourself what your team have to do if the company and the team are to reach the goals. During this phase, you'll identify the "performance gap" between what your team can do now, and what they must be able to do.
- Determine the training activities that will help the team learn to perform the tasks and will empower them to achieve their own personal goals. This will include all areas including product knowledge, customer service training, management training (for those wanting to move up the ranks or already in a position of authority)

Step two is to remember your team are adults, and not children.
Adults:
- Are self-directed
- Come to training with a lifetime of existing knowledge, experience, and opinions
- Are goal-oriented

- Want training that is relevant
- Want training that is task-oriented
- Learn when they see "what's in it for them"
- Want to be and feel respected

Step three: Before you begin creating any training, it's critical that you create a list of learning objectives.

Learning objectives are a list of things the team members must be able to do after the training is completed. Once you've created your learning objectives, create content that covers the objectives—and nothing but. In addition, any quizzes, tests, case studies, or hands-on exercises performed during training to evaluate your teams understanding of the training. Evaluating the training can also be done once it is in practice within the business.

Make your learning objectives SMART:
When you write an objective, it should have five characteristics, known collectively by the acronym

SMART.
Specific, Measurable, Achieveable, Relevant and Timebound.

Step Four is to either design your training, or have an expert do it for you. Larger companies will have a training department which can do this for you, however, many companies do not have the finances to do this for themselves and will outsource.

Steps one and three are really something a leader should decide upon for themselves. The team around you are the ones that are going to help you achieve the vision of the company, and therefore the training is imperative to not only achieve the company vision, but also to help the team stay motivated and looking after your customers on a daily basis in a positive and business building way.

Training should always be interactive, and keep teams interested.

But, just because you have trained the team, it doesn't stop there.

Holding one on one reviews with the team is very important. It gives you the opportunity to get to know your team members, to tell them the positives of what they are doing and be able to praise them and to give constructive feedback on what they need to work on to improve themselves. This in turn will improve your business.

Your company might have set timeframes in which to perform these reviews, but if they don't, it is good practice to do these on a regular basis, at least quarterly.

Whether it's a performance review, a salary adjustment meeting, or the implementation of a performance review plan, these tips will help you more confidently lead the meeting.

These tips are applicable in your daily conversations with team members. They are also critical in your formal meetings with team members to discuss job goals and performance. The following should help you make performance reviews positive and motivational. They will improve your ability to interact with your team members and help your business to flourish.

1. Performance Review Tips

The team member should never hear about positive performance or performance in need of improvement for the first time at your formal performance discussion meeting unless it is new information or insight. Great leaders discuss both positive performance and areas for improvement regularly, even daily or weekly. Aim to make the contents of the performance review discussion a re-emphasis of critical points.

In the interest of providing regular feedback, performance reviews are not an annual event. Quarterly meetings are recommended with team members.

It doesn't matter what your performance review process is, the first step is goal setting. It is imperative that the team member knows exactly what is expected of his or her performance. Your periodic discussions about performance need to focus on these significant portions of the team members job.

You need to document this job plan: goals and expectations in a job plan or job expectations format. Without a written agreement and a shared picture of the team members goals, success for the team member or your business is unlikely.

2. Sharing Performance Review Format

Make sure that you also share the performance review format with the team member, so they is not surprised at the end of the performance review time period. A significant component of this evaluation discussion is to share with them how the company and yourself will assess performance.

3. Get Feedback

Get feedback from other team members who have worked closely with the person you are holding the review with. Sometimes called 360-degree feedback because you are obtaining feedback for the team member from their boss, coteam members, and any reporting staff, you use the feedback to broaden the performance information that you provide for them.

Start with informal discussions to obtain feedback information. Consider developing a format so that the feedback is easy to digest and share with the manager. If your company uses a form that you fill out in advance of the meeting, give the performance review to the team member in advance of the meeting. This allows the team member to digest the contents before her discussion of the details with you. This simple gesture can remove a lot of the emotion and drama from the performance review meeting.

4. Preparing for a Discussion

Prepare for the discussion with the team member. Never go into a performance review without preparation. If you wing it, performance reviews fail. You will miss key opportunities for feedback and improvement, and the team member will not feel

encouraged about their successes.
The documentation that you maintained during the performance review period serves you well as you prepare for an team member's performance review.

5. Meeting with a Team member

When you meet with the team member, spend time on the positive aspects of his or her performance. In most cases, the discussion of the positive components of the team member's performance should take up more time than that of the negative components.

For your above average performing team members and your performing team members, positive feedback and discussion about how the team member can continue to grow her performance should comprise the majority of the discussion. The team member will find this rewarding and motivating.

No team member's performance is completely negative—if so, why does the team member still work for your company? But, don't neglect the areas that need improvement either. Especially for an underperforming team member, speak directly and don't mince words. If you are not direct, the team member will not understand the seriousness of the performance situation. Use examples from the whole time period covered by the performance review.

6. Conversation is Key to a Productive Meeting

The spirit in which you approach this conversation will make the difference in whether it is effective. If your intention is genuine, to help the team member improve, and you have a positive relationship with the team member, the conversation is easier and more effective.

The team member has to trust that you want to help them improve their performance. They need to hear you say that you have confidence in their ability to improve. This helps them believe that they have the ability and the support necessary to improve.

Conversation is the keyword when you define a performance review meeting. If you are doing all of the talking or the meeting becomes a lecture, the performance review is less effective.

You want an team member who is motivated and excited about their ability to continue to grow, develop, and contribute.

Aim for performance review meetings in which the team member talks more than half of the time. You can encourage this conversation by asking questions such as these.

- What do you expect to be the most challenging about your goals for this quarter?

- What support can the department provide for you that will help you reach these goals?

- What are your hopes for your achievements at our company this year?

- How can I be a better manager for you?

- How often would you like to receive feedback?

- What kind of schedule can we set up so that you don't feel micromanaged, but I receive the feedback that I need as to your progress on your goals?

- What would be a helpful agenda for our weekly one-on-one meetings?

If you take these performance review tips to heart and practice these recommendations in your performance review meetings, you will develop a significant tool for your leadership abilities. The performance review can enhance your relationship with team members, improve performance for your company, and enhance team member-manager communication significantly—a boon for customers and work relationships.

A sample review document I have used in the past is below

Team member Review

What do you believe has been the area you've developed in most in your role since your last review and why?

What do you believe are your main strengths that you bring to the role and why?

What has been your most significant or difficult challenge since your last review and why?

What has been your greatest success since your last review and why?

What development, if any, have you undertaken since your last review and how have you applied what you have learned in the work place?

What development do you feel would benefit you and the business in the next quarter?

What are your short term and long term career aspirations? How may I support you to achieve these?

What are your key objectives (areas of focus) for the next quarter?

What were your key objectives (areas of focus) for this quarter and how have you achieved them?

I always found having the team fill out their own review prior to sitting down with them, also gave a true indication of their needs and future goals. It gave the team members ownership of the review process, and meant the review was not an awkward moment in time, when the team member did not know how to answer a question. It empowered them.

Try hard to hold reviews at least quarterly. This means some of the goals set at each review can be kept small, which helps the team member achieve them. This will in turn motivate them to learn and achieve more over time.

EMPOWERING YOUR TEAM

Empowerment is defined as *"the giving or delegation of power or authority; authorization; the giving of an ability; enablement or permission."*

What is the point of growing yourself as a leader, creating a great vision for your business, training your teams and putting lots of time and effort into building the best team you can possibly have if you do not empower them?

There are so many examples of leaders who do not empower their teams, it is hard to know where to begin.

I would be lying if I said during my career I had always empowered my teams. I have been through phases where I have felt let down by teams, stolen from and more, which in turn, made me more of a bad leader at the time. It becomes a viscious cycle, the trust on both sides goes, and customer service suffers.

However, I have learnt that business can flourish, as well as the team members when you empower your team. It takes the pressure off you as a leader to feel that you have to do everything yourself, frees up your time to keep building on the business and team around you, and gives your customers the ability to have all of their issues resolved immediately, giving them faith in your company and products.

I have found there are many more advantages to empowering your team members, some of which are listed below.

1) **Team members are more accountable**

When team members are empowered, they have to accept responsibility. They can no longer claim, "that's not my job." They don't have the luxury of shirking work because they're autonomous. They have the resources and the authority to step up and take action.

2) Team members are more attentive

Because team members are empowered, they cannot be asleep at their posts. They must be ready and reactive because they are able to make a difference. Empowered team members can even be proactive and recognize when there are small issues that need to be solved. This prevents small issues from turning into big problems.

3) Team members will feel more valued

Empowering your team members shows that they are trusted. Team members who feel valued and trusted tend to be more engaged. ***Studies suggest that companies with engaged team members outperform those without by up to 202%.*** Engaged team members are more likely to use discretionary effort—to go above and beyond—to impact the customer experience.

4) Team members will be more invested in their work

Empowered team members recognize that their decisions are contributing to the company's success and consequently, they care more about their work. Additionally, they can express initiative and creativity without asking permission from a superior, and this allows them to feel a pride of ownership in their work.

5) Problems are resolved faster
According to a survey commissioned by LivePerson, *"82% of consumers say the number one factor that leads to a great customer service experience is having their issues resolved quickly."*

When team members are not empowered, customers must work their way up the chain of command in order to get their problems resolved. Often times they have to wait while someone in a position of higher authority is located, and sometimes your upset customers must repeat their sad story to several people. Waiting and repetition do not lead to happy customers. Empowered team members can resolve issues immediately—eliminating the need for repetition and waiting.

6) Customers experience better service

As already discussed, empowered team members tend to be more engaged, more proactive, more attentive to customers and more invested in their work. Is it any wonder that all of this leads to a better customer experience? When team members enjoy their work, they share that joy with their customers.

How can you ensure your Teams feel empowered? Teams can only be empowered if you allow them to feel empowered. Some leaders will find this a hard thing to do, as they feel as though they are 'letting go' of control (I know, I was one of them).

Learn to let go. The biggest problem most new leaders face is the inability to let go of their own work. Sometimes they feel so dedicated to completing their own work that they refuse to let other people help. Other times, they fear that nobody else has the skills or abilities necessary to execute the work effectively.

Whatever the case may be, your first priority needs to be to learn to let go. Start small, empowering your teams only the smallest tasks, and gradually work your way up. Get to know your team better and improve the trust among you and your team members. Take baby steps and know that eventually you will have to let go of your work if you want your team to be successful.

Establish a firm priority system. As part of the letting-go process, start developing a priority system for tasks. Of course, this system will vary on the basis of your expertise, your industry, and the types of tasks you usually handle, but create at least four categories, according to the degree of effort a task requires and the degree of skill. The highest-skilled category should contain tasks that you keep on your own plate, while those in the lower-skilled categories can be assigned to others.

The degree of effort should tell you which tasks are more important to delegate--for example, giving someone else responsibility for a high-effort, low-skill task will save you lots of time.

Play to your teams strengths. You should know each individual's strengths and weaknesses, including his or her current, and potential, range of skills. When empowering, take a look at your team and assign tasks to whoever has the greatest number of relevant skills for that task. It seems like an obvious choice, but too many leaders delegate to whoever has the lightest workload or is the most convenient.

It's also important to be consistent. For example, empowering the same type of tasks to the same individual will eventually increase that individual's aptitude for those tasks.

Always include instructions. Even if the task process seems obvious to you, make sure to include instructions with each task you delegate. If you have specific preferences for how the assignment will be carried out, include that information. If you have a strict deadline or milestones you need to hit, be clear about them.

Including details and straightforward instructions from the get-go will avoid most communication gaps and will allow your tasks to be executed effectively. It's a proactive strategy that both you and your employees will appreciate.

Don't be afraid to teach new skills. Lacking someone on your team with the ability to execute a certain task on your to-do list doesn't mean the work can't be delegated. Most skills can be learned--some more easily than others--so don't be afraid to teach as a part of the delegation process.

Though the assignment of your first few tasks will take more time than it will save you (since you'll need to train your chosen employee), consider it an investment. By transferring those skills, you'll be opening the door to assigning all similar tasks to that individual in the future, ultimately saving more time than you spent teaching.

Trust, but always check. Once a task is delegated, trust your teams to execute it on his or her own terms. This will allow the person to tackle the work the way they feel is best. However, don't be afraid to occasionally step in and verify that the task is moving along as planned.

For example, if you made an assignment a week ago that's due tomorrow, trust that your employee is on top of things, but send a quick verification email to make sure the person hasn't hit any snags.

Doing so encourages more trust and respect within your team and helps prevent breaks in communication or understanding.

Use feedback to improve empowerment moving forward. Feedback is the most important part of the empowering process, and it works both ways. If your team members have done well with a task you assigned, let them know by publicly thanking them and offering genuine praise. If they've fallen short, don't be afraid to give them some constructive criticism.

On the other hand, invite your team members to share their thoughts on how you're empowering--it's a critical chance for you to determine whether you're providing enough information, or whether you're assigning the right tasks to the right people.

Empowering isn't always easy, and the process isn't always clear cut, but the sooner you start, the sooner you'll develop the expertise to do it effectively. Realize that the process will never be perfect but learn from your experiences and make ongoing adjustments for improvement.

Empowering your team can be as simple as allowing them to be able to replace a customers meal if the customer has made a complaint. This empowerment alone will ensure your customer has their problem resolved quickly and is considered by the customer to have been handled well, instead of them having to wait for a manager to have a moment to deal with it. If your team has been trained well, they will be able to handle this type of incident easily.

Some great examples of team empowerment can be seen in these two examples:

Timpson – Share the power
John Timpson's Upside Down Management principle has been well documented. He has been empowering his team for decades and has published successful books on his practices.

He provides a thorough training scheme and gives his colleagues access up to £500 to solve customer issues before they need authorisation from a manager. This means they can resolve the issues quickly and efficiently while feeling trusted to do so.

Disney – Reward Good Work
Disney are world renowned for their guest experience, with 'cast members' working to ensure every touch point is magical. One way they empower their staff is through a simple demonstration of genuine care.

They make sure they thank their staff, they listen to them for unique opportunities to take action or provide reasoned responses and they share positive customer stories. People naturally want to be successful and being rewarded in even the simplest ways encourages and reinforces these positive attributes.

You could take this further and create a reward scheme such as extra days off, financial bonuses or special event tickets.

MANAGING CONFLICT

As companies continue to restructure work teams and grow, the need for training in conflict resolution will grow. Conflict arises from differences, and when individuals come together in teams, their differences in terms of power, values, and attitudes contribute to the creation of conflict.

To avoid the negative results on your team and business that can result from disagreements, most methods of resolving conflict is the importance of dealing with disputes quickly and openly. Conflict is not necessarily destructive, however. When managed properly, conflict can result in benefits for a team.

Resolving Conflict in Work Teams

A major advantage a team has over an individual is its diversity of resources, knowledge, and ideas. However, diversity also produces conflict. Varney (1989) reports that conflict remained the number-one problem for most of the teams operating within a large or small company, even after repeated training sessions on how to resolve conflict and how to minimize the negative impact on team members.

One reason for this may be that leaders within companies are not giving the issue of resolving conflict enough attention. Varney's research showed that although most leaders are aware of disagreements and have received training in conflict resolution, they seldom assign a high priority to solving conflict problems.

With this in mind, it is critical that team members possess skills to resolve conflict among themselves. Conflict arises from differences. When individuals come together in work teams their differences in terms of power, values and attitudes, and social factors all contribute to the creation of conflict. It is often difficult to expose the sources of conflict.

Conflict can arise from numerous sources within a team setting and generally falls into three categories: communication factors, structural factors and personal factors (Varney, 1989).

Communication is among the most important factors and can be a major source of misunderstanding.

Communication barriers include poor listening skills; insufficient sharing of information; differences in interpretation and perception; and nonverbal cues being ignored or missed. Structural disagreements include the size of the company, turnover rate, levels of participation, reward systems, and differing levels on empowerment among team members.

Personal factors include things such as an individual's self-esteem, their personal goals, values and needs. Nelson (1995) cautions that negative conflict can destroy a team quickly, and often arises from poor planning. He offers this list of high potential areas from which negative conflict issues commonly arise:

If the team lacks good groundwork for what it's doing, its members will not be able to coordinate their work.
This brings us onto team shortages. If the team does not have enough people to do the job, it is inevitable that some will carry too heavy a load. Resentment may build, so it is important leaders are aware and action any shortages.

This is particularly prevalent in Customer service industries, as the pressure upon the team can become too much for the team to handle, which again results in poor service and losses in sales.

Overspend in certain areas of the business can also cause conflict between the team. Often inevitable, overspends become a problem when proper measures are not taken. Especially if one department spends more than another, the resentment will slowly build if this is not addressed immediately. This way the problem can be resolved before it grows into a problem for the entire team and the business.

The timeframe for various actions' within the business should be highly visible. All members should be willing to work together to help each other meet their deadlines. A great example of this is within the hospitality industry. This over the years has caused a great deal of grief, due to leaders not communicating exact timeframes from their kitchen team, leaving the front of house team giving 'false promises' to the customer. This in turn can make the customer very unhappy with the service.
Stick to the Vision at hand and avoid being sidetracked into trying to fit other things into it. Wait and do the other things you would like to do after succeeding with the Vision first.

Team members as well as leaders can and should attempt to avoid negative conflict from occurring. Being aware of the potential for negative conflict to occur and taking the necessary steps to ensure good planning will help.

Handling Negative Conflict

When negative conflict does occur there are five accepted methods for handling it: Direct Approach, Bargaining, Enforcement, Retreat, and De-emphasis (Nelson, 1995). Each can be used effectively in different circumstances.

1. Direct Approach: This may be the best approach of all. It concentrates on the leader confronting the issue head-on. Though conflict is uncomfortable to deal with, it is best to look at issues objectively and to face them as they are. If criticism is used, it must be constructive to the recipients. This approach counts on the techniques of problem-solving and normally leaves everyone with a sense of resolution, because issues are brought to the surface and dealt with.

2. Bargaining: This is an excellent technique when both parties have ideas on a solution yet cannot find common ground. Often a third party, such as a team leader, is needed to help find the compromise. Compromise involves give and take on both sides, however, and usually ends up with both walking away equally dissatisfied.

3. Enforcement of Team Rules: Avoid using this method if possible, it can bring about hard feelings toward the leader and the team. This technique is only used when it is obvious that a member does not want to be a team player and refuses to work with the rest. If enforcement has to be used on an individual, it may be best for that person to find another team.

4. Retreat: Only use this method when the problem isn't real to begin with. By simply avoiding it or working around it, a leader can often delay long enough for the individual to cool off. When used in the right environment by an experienced leader this technique can help to prevent minor incidents that are the result of someone having a bad day from becoming real problems that should never have occurred.

5. De-emphasis: This is a form of bargaining where the emphasis is on the areas of agreement. When parties realize that there are areas where they are in agreement, they can often begin to move in a new direction.

All this said, management of conflict is just not restricted to the team.

Conflicts with Customers can be one of the biggest challenges within business.
It can be hard to not respond in a negative way, especially when you put your heart and soul into your business and your teams.

I remember being told once that you should not get emotional when a customer 'has a go'. Well, this can be a very hard thing to do, and personally, I believe if you do not get upset when a customer complains, then your heart is not in it.

Customer service employees can experience conflict with customers on a fairly regular basis, depending on the industry. A common conflict experienced by salespeople is a dissatisfied customer who feels personally defrauded by an individual salesperson.

For example, if a car salesman sells a used car without a performance guarantee or warranty and the car breaks down on the buyer, the buyer may return to angrily confront the salesperson and demand a refund. The best first step to solve these conflicts is to involve a manager who has the right to offer refunds, discounts or other conciliatory gestures to the customer unless you are in a situation where employees are empowered to make these kinds of decisions.

Leadership Conflicts are more common with leaders who do not try to improve themselves continuously. Personality clashes between leaders and teams can cause a range of conflicts to arise. Teams may feel bullied or pushed by more authoritarian leaders or may perceive a lack of guidance from more hands-off Leaders. Some leaders may set goals that are too ambitious for their teams, setting them up for failure and inevitable conflict.

Managing team conflict is an important part of leading your team to success and needs to be something your take 'head on' and not hide from, before the problem gets worse.

FINAL THOUGHTS

I am still learning every day how to become a better leader. Anyone who tells you there is such a thing as a 'perfect leader' is just kidding themselves.

The best of the best are always learning, always finding new ways to lead their teams and businesses to success. The world is moving very quickly, and customers expectations keep getting higher and higher, meaning we as leaders have to keep moving ourselves forward at all times.

So take the challenge:

DECIDE TO BECOME A BETTER LEADER

CREATE A VISION THAT WILL TAKE YOU, YOUR TEAM AND YOUR BUSINESS TO THE NEXT LEVEL

CREATE A GREAT TEAM

SET YOUR STANDARDS

EMPOWER YOUR TEAM

and finally, MANAGE YOUR TEAM CONFLICT.

I have decided to become a better leader...have you?

www.ingramcontent.com/pod-product-compliance
Lightning Source LLC
Chambersburg PA
CBHW071206220526
45468CB00002B/521